First World War
and Army of Occupation
War Diary
France, Belgium and Germany

41 DIVISION
Divisional Troops
Royal Army Veterinary Corps
52 Mobile Veterinary Section
31 May 1916 - 30 October 1917

WO95/2630/4

The Naval & Military Press Ltd
www.nmarchive.com
Published in association with The National Archives

Published by

The Naval & Military Press Ltd

Unit 10 Ridgewood Industrial Park,

Uckfield, East Sussex,

TN22 5QE England

Tel: +44 (0) 1825 749494

www.naval-military-press.com

www.nmarchive.com

This diary has been reprinted in facsimile from the original. Any imperfections are inevitably reproduced and the quality may fall short of modern type and cartographic standards.

© **Crown Copyright**
Images reproduced by permission of The National Archives, London, England, 2015.

Contents

Document type	Place/Title	Date From	Date To
Heading	WO95/2630/4 May 1916-Oct 1917 52 Mobile Veterinary Section		
Heading	52nd Mobile-Very Sect. May 1916-Oct 1917 1918 Mar-1919 Oct. 1 Italy 1917 Nov-1918 Feb		
War Diary	Nieppe	31/05/1916	31/05/1916
Heading	War Diary For June 1916 R Daubney Capt-A.V.C 52nd Mobile Veterinary Section		
War Diary	36. B8.d.3.6	16/06/1916	26/06/1916
Heading	War Diary For July 1916 R Daubney Capt. A.V.C. O.C 52nd Mobile Veterinary Section		
War Diary	Sheet 36. B8.d4.6.	12/07/1916	18/08/1916
War Diary	Sheet 36 A16a66.	19/08/1916	19/08/1916
War Diary	Cocquerel	24/08/1916	24/08/1916
War Diary	Epagne	25/08/1916	05/09/1916
War Diary	St Etoile	06/09/1916	06/09/1916
War Diary	St Sauveur	07/09/1916	07/09/1916
War Diary	Buire. Sur-L'Ancre	11/09/1916	11/09/1916
War Diary	Albert	13/09/1916	18/09/1916
War Diary	Ribemont	19/09/1916	29/09/1916
War Diary	Mametz	30/09/1916	15/10/1916
War Diary	Buire-Sur-L'Ancre	16/10/1916	16/10/1916
War Diary	Argoeuves	17/10/1916	17/10/1916
War Diary	Longpre	18/10/1916	20/10/1916
War Diary	Caestre	21/10/1916	21/10/1916
War Diary	Fletre	23/10/1916	23/10/1916
War Diary	Reninghelst.	24/10/1916	26/10/1916
War Diary	Reninghelst. G32D81	01/11/1916	30/12/1916
War Diary	Reninghelst. G32D81 Sheet 28.	02/01/1917	29/01/1917
War Diary	Reninghelst. G32D8.1	01/02/1917	28/02/1917
War Diary	Reninghelst. Sheet 28 G32D.8.1.	01/03/1917	31/03/1917
War Diary	Reninghelst. G32d.8.1.	04/04/1917	28/04/1917
War Diary	G32d8.1 Reninghelst	01/05/1917	31/05/1917
War Diary	Reninghelst G32d8.1.	01/06/1917	14/06/1917
War Diary	La Clytte	14/06/1917	29/06/1917
Heading	War Diary Of July 1917 O.C 52nd Mobile Veterinary Section		
War Diary	La Clytte Nya 85.	01/07/1917	01/07/1917
War Diary	Berthen R216.1.3	02/07/1917	25/07/1917
War Diary	La. Clytte N7a8.6.	24/07/1917	31/07/1917
War Diary	La Clytte N7a8.5	02/08/1917	14/08/1917
War Diary	Berthen R.21.b.13.	16/08/1917	16/08/1917
War Diary	Berthen	19/08/1917	21/08/1917
War Diary	Wizernes	27/08/1917	14/09/1917
War Diary	Berthen	15/09/1917	15/09/1917
War Diary	La Clytte	16/09/1917	23/09/1917
War Diary	Caestre	24/09/1917	27/09/1917
War Diary	Leffrin Koucke	27/09/1917	29/09/1917
War Diary	W.26.Central	01/10/1917	03/10/1917
War Diary	La Panne	04/10/1917	07/10/1917
War Diary	St. Idesbalde.	08/10/1917	30/10/1917

WO95/2630

May 1916 – Oct 1917

52 Mobile Veterinary Section

(4)

41ST DIVISION

FRANCE

52ND MOBILE VETY SECN.

MAY 1916 — ~~DEC 1918~~ 1917 OCT

1918 MAR — 1919 OCT

ITALY 1917 NOV — 1918 FEB

Box 2630

52. M.Vet.Sn

Army Form C. 2118.

WAR DIARY
or
INTELLIGENCE SUMMARY.
(Erase heading not required.)

Place	Date	Hour	Summary of Events and Information	Remarks and references to Appendices
Neppe	3.5.16	6.4pm	The section left Aldershot on the 4-5-16 by special troop train & embarked the same evening at Southampton, arriving at Havre 10 am 5.5.16, where disembarkation was accomplished without any untoward occurrence. Proceeded thru to Rest Camp No 2, Sauvic, Divisional Camby. On the 7-5-16 entrained at Havre with Divisional Camby. Sanitary Section & detrained at Caestre 8.5.16, proceeding by road to Borre. The normal duties & functions of a Mobile Veterinary Section commenced at Borre on the 9.5.16. The section left Borre on the 17.6 & proceeded by road to a billet about 1 mile west of Neppe in the Neppe - Bailleul road — Sheet 36. B 8 d 3,6. where it remains at the present moment. The Hdq̃s was taken over from the 31st Mobile Veterinary Section, & has been standing over for the section horses, the	

Army Form C. 2118.

WAR DIARY
or
INTELLIGENCE SUMMARY.
(Erase heading not required.)

Instructions regarding War Diaries and Intelligence Summaries are contained in F. S. Regs., Part II. and the Staff Manual respectively. Title pages will be prepared in manuscript.

Place	Date	Hour	Summary of Events and Information	Remarks and references to Appendices
No. II Sheet	31.5.16		Lines however requiring considerable repair. Accommodation of sick horses there was a field roughly 100 feet square, with a small standing to accommodate 6 horses. Further standings could not be laid down owing to the difficulty in obtaining material. A part of the adjoining clover field was taken as the most suitable place for isolation & there it was decided to picket any horses which required isolation. The men were billeted comfortably in one G.S. hut & in a large barn.	
			RH Aubrey Capt AVC for O.C. 53rd Mobile Veterinary Section	

War Diary
for June 1916

R Daubney Capt. A.V.C

52nd Mobile Veterinary Section

Army Form C. 2118.

WAR DIARY
or
INTELLIGENCE SUMMARY.
(Erase heading not required.)

Place	Date	Hour	Summary of Events and Information	Remarks and references to Appendices
1st Sheet				
36.B8.a.3.6	16.6.16	6 p.m.	Command of the Section was taken over by Captain R. DAUBNEY A.V.C. (S.R.) from Lieut E.J.B. SEWELL A.V.C. (T.C.).	
do	17.6.16	2 a.m	Gas alarm sounded from region about due EAST. Wind about N.E. by T. very light. Troops leading animals, seen passing along road from direction of NIEPPE towards BAILLEUL, were ordered to put on helmets. So about 1 gas seen approaching, moving in a direction at right angles to BAILLEUL-NIEPPE ROAD. About 12-45 a.m. a further gas alarm was sounded, & in view of the fact that this probably meant a further release of gas, the men were ordered to lead all horses down the BAILLEUL-NIEPPE Rd. towards BAILLEUL. The gas in the region of the Section's billet was by this time moderately thick, & several horses were coughing. A halt was made beyond PONT D'ACHELLES when the road was quite clear of gas, the edge of the gas cloud being some 200 yards further EAST along the road. The second alarm was evidently a false one	

Army Form C. 2118.

WAR DIARY
or
INTELLIGENCE SUMMARY.
(Erase heading not required.)

Place	Date	Hour	Summary of Events and Information	Remarks and references to Appendices
2nd Sheet			As in about half an hour, the part of the road adjacent to the billet was seen to be clearing. The road becoming clear the section returned to billets at about 1.30 a.m. Saw lame horse & a mare in foal were left behind at the billet when party moved on. The lame horse did not suffer, but the mare foaled prematurely about an hour later, whether this was due to gas or to the excitement caused by the other horses being seen to leave the billet is a point not easily decided. It was remarked that on exit where mules were totted down the road through the gas cloud had several animals gassed, but all recovered. Other units much nearer the place of origin of gas cloud whose horses were not moved, suffered no ill effect.	
As above	17.6.16	11.15pm	Gas alarm. Wind N.N.W. & alarm came from N.E., so ordered guard to call me in event of men were to sleep, & ordered guard to call me in event of	

T2134. Wt. W708—776. 50000. 4/15. Sr J. C. & S.

WAR DIARY
or
INTELLIGENCE SUMMARY.
(Erase heading not required.)

Army Form C. 2118.

Place	Date	Hour	Summary of Events and Information	Remarks and references to Appendices
3rd Sheep			Any further alarm, or alteration in direction of wind. Nothing further reported.	
As above.	19.6.16	2am	Gas alarm. Wind N.E. Probably false. Turned in.	
	23.6.16	6pm	This afternoon took three animals to Gaunt School. One animal gassed for quarter of an hour in steady stream of chlorine, whilst wearing helmet. Animal was of particularly phlegmatic temperament & stood perfectly quietly, showed no after effects whatever. A rather more nervous animal refused to stand wearing a helmet, & became very excited, & helmet had to be removed. A third animal was subjected to about "same amount" of gas as first, the horse coughed a few times while in the gas. All animals walked quietly home, about three miles, all three fed well. It was noticed that animal subjected to gas without helmet coughed moderately, & temperature was 103. Other normal.	
	24.6.16	5pm	The animal gassed without helmet was normal this morning. Lu temperature	

Army Form C. 2118.

WAR DIARY
or
INTELLIGENCE SUMMARY.
(Erase heading not required.)

Place	Date	Hour	Summary of Events and Information	Remarks and references to Appendices
1st Sheet			T coughed occasionally when feeding. No further ill effects here present. It was noted that during the experimental wearing of helmet, differences was caused by material of helmet flapping & leaving belt around nostrils.	
As above	26.4.16 6pm		Animals evacuated by road to St OMER & No 23 Veterinary Hospital. 5 cases DEBILITY & 1 shell wound. These animals reached destination without untoward occurrence.	

R.D. Aubrey Capt A.V.C.
O.C. 3rd Mob Vety Sec

41 10 July

52. M.V. Sec
Vol 2

War Diary for June 1916

R Dawbney Capt. A.V.C.
O.C 52nd Mobile Veterinary Section

WAR DIARY
or
INTELLIGENCE SUMMARY.

Army Form C. 2118.

Place	Date	Hour	Summary of Events and Information	Remarks and references to Appendices
Sheet 36. B6 a4.4	6/7/16		Evacuation by barge to St OMER No. 23 Veterinary Hospital began this day, the barges leaving from La Gorgue, near ESTAIRES.	
—	10/7/16		This day evacuation of Class A cases by road commenced. The party made the journey without any untoward incident.	
—	16/7/16		Reconnoitred a position for Advanced Aid Post in case of increased activity necessitating the Section being moved back. Decided on Site at B11.D.4.6. near (Ooten) OOSTHOVE FARM.	
—	19/7/16		Place of Embarkation of Class B cases changed to BAC ST MAUR, which is much more convenient for this Section.	

R. Dauberg Capt AVC
O.C. 52nd Mobile Veterinary Section

VOL 3

Army Form C. 2118.

52nd Mobile V.C.H. Section

WAR DIARY
or
INTELLIGENCE SUMMARY.
(Erase heading not required.)

Instructions regarding War Diaries and Intelligence Summaries are contained in F. S. Regs., Part II. and the Staff Manual respectively. Title pages will be prepared in manuscript.

Place	Date	Hour	Summary of Events and Information	Remarks and references to Appendices
Shot-36 A.B. d.4.6	18.8.16	—	Marched at 10 a.m. under orders to a billet previously reconnoitred at Shot 36 A.16 a.6 of STEENVERCK. Handed over sick horses to M.V.S. 23rd Division. Billeted men in fields, men in farm.	
" 36 A.16.a.6	19.8.16		Reft billets at STEENVERCK 2.30 a.m. to arrive	
COQUEREL	24.8.16		WEST STATION at 3.30 A.M. to entrain. Entrained detachment (complete) without difficulty, being first detachment to arrive. Train left 6-40 arrived PONT REMY at 3 P.M. Detrained first of train & proceeded to billets at COQUEREL, arriving at 6-40 P.M. Accommodation for horses first good, & no place for sick horse. Rodded to charge of books.	
EPAGNE	26.8.16	—	Searched with Staff Captain R.A. for more convenient billets & found one in EPAGNE. Troops in the open on hillside, men in own empty horse.	
do.	30.6.16		In view of the inclemency of the weather exposed	

WAR DIARY
or
INTELLIGENCE SUMMARY.
(Erase heading not required.)

Army Form C. 2118.

Place	Date	Hour	Summary of Events and Information	Remarks and references to Appendices
as above			Section of horses moved down & arranged to billet them in the stables & grounds of house where men are billeted. Would express opinion that on the day of a train journey the hay ration might be increased with advantage, as the consumption of hay keeps animals quiet in the boxes.	

D Whitney Capt RAVC
O.C. 52nd Mobile Veterinary Section

Army Form C. 2118.

37 MVS, Vol 4

WAR DIARY
or
INTELLIGENCE SUMMARY.
(Erase heading not required.)

Instructions regarding War Diaries and Intelligence Summaries are contained in F. S. Regs., Part II. and the Staff Manual respectively. Title pages will be prepared in manuscript.

Place	Date	Hour	Summary of Events and Information	Remarks and references to Appendices
EPAGNE	5/9/16	—	Command of the section was taken over by Capt. C.W.B. Sites A.V.C. from Capt. R. Bartley A.V.C. (S.R.) The section left EPAGNE, marching under orders of 12th Infantry Bde. and proceeded to S⁺ ETOILE where it halted for the night. All horses were tied on a line in an open field, the NCOs and men being billetted in a barn.	
S⁺ ETOILE	6/9/16		The section left S⁺ ETOINE on this day and marched to S⁺ SAUVEUR where they bivouacked for the night in an open field.	
S⁺ SAUVEUR	7/9/16		The section left S⁺ SAUVEUR on this day and marched to BUIRE-SUR-L'ANCRE bivouacking in an open field.	
BUIRE-SUR-L'ANCRE	11/9/16		Evacuated 29 horses and 1 mule from MERICOURT station to No.7 Veterinary Hospital FORGES-LES-EAUX	
do	do		The section left BUIRE-SUR-L'ANCRE on this day, marching to ALBERT where they bivouacked on the ALBERT & VILLIERS MILL Road	
ALBERT	13/9/16		On this day No. S.E. 540 Pte/Serg⁺ R.G. MELROSE A.V.C. was reverted to his permanent grade for inefficiency.	

WAR DIARY
or
INTELLIGENCE SUMMARY.
(Erase heading not required.)

Army Form C. 2118.

Date	Hour	Summary of Events and Information	Remarks and references to Appendices
ALBERT 13.9.16		*Sheet 2* Authority D.D.V.S. 1st Army No.1466, dated 9.9.16, and was posted to No.2 Base Veterinary Hospital, HAVRE, for duty.	
do.	13.9.16	Evacuated 21 horses and 3 mules to No.7 Veterinary Hospital from EDGEHILL Station.	
		An advanced Veterinary Collecting Station for wounded horses was established at 6 A.M. for this date at A.3.a.8.2.	
do.	16.9.16	Evacuated 9 horses and 2 mules to No.7 Veterinary Hospital from EDGEHILL Station.	
do.	17.9.16	The advanced Veterinary Collecting Station was closed on this date.	
do.	18.9.16	Evacuated 10 horses to No.4 Veterinary Hospital from EDGEHILL Station.	
do.	18.9.16	The Section left ALBERT and Proceeded to RIBEMONT, where they were billeted on a Farm with the 41st Divisional M.M.P. one standing for the horses was good, and accn for NCO's and men.	
RIBEMONT 19.9.16		No.772 P/A/Sergt B.LONG joined the section from No.8 Veterinary Hospital	

Army Form C. 2118.

WAR DIARY
or
INTELLIGENCE SUMMARY.
(Erase heading not required.)

Instructions regarding War Diaries and Intelligence Summaries are contained in F. S. Regs., Part II. and the Staff Manual respectively. Title pages will be prepared in manuscript.

Place	Date	Hour	Summary of Events and Information	Remarks and references to Appendices
			Sheet 3	
RIBEMONT	19.9.16		O/C Head sent Embryo to No.46 Mobile Veterinary Section, in accordance with D.D.V.S. 4th Army, Letter No.1546, dated 19.9.16	
do	22.9.16		Evacuated 12 horses and 2 mules to No.7 Veterinary Hospital from MERICOURT Station.	
do.	25.9.16		Evacuated 13 horses and 4 mules to No.7 Veterinary Hospital from Mericourt Station	
do.	28.9.16		Evacuated 7 horses and 3 mules to No.7 Veterinary Hospital from MERICOURT Station	
do.	29.9.16		O/C section left RIBEMONT and marched to MAMETZ and bivouacked there.	
MAMETZ	30.9.16		Admitted 15 horses from 1st Divisional Artillery	
do.	30.9.16		One Pmr. A.V.C. sent for temporary duty to Wrecking Mobile Veterinary Section MEAULTE.	

CWOhikes
Capt. A.V.C.
O.C. 52nd Mobile Veterinary Section

Army Form C. 2118.

Vol S

WAR DIARY
or
INTELLIGENCE SUMMARY.
(Erase heading not required.)

Instructions regarding War Diaries and Intelligence Summaries are contained in F. S. Regs., Part II. and the Staff Manual respectively. Title pages will be prepared in manuscript.

Place	Date	Hour	Summary of Events and Information	Remarks and references to Appendices
MAMETZ	1/10/16	1st Oct	No. S.E. 8390 Pte E. HAYNES admitted to Hospital at FORGES-LES-EAUX, when one of a conducting party of sick horses.	
"	1/10/16		Discharged one H.D. to Fo. 1 Coy. A.S.C. Cured of skin disease	
"			Discharged one stray mule to F.10 R.W. Kent Rgt. 123 Infy. Bde.	
"			Discharged 9 horses to 20 Durham L. Infy. 123 Infy. Bde. & issued Brushes &c.	
"			Evacuated 15 horses to collecting M.V.S. at MEAULTE.	
"	2/10/16		Evacuated 35 horses & 4 mules to collecting M.V.S. at MEAULTE.	
"	3/10/16		Evacuated 15 horses & 3 mules to collecting M.V.S. at MEAULTE.	
"			Destroyed the horse belonging to 76 Bde. R.F.A., 14th Division, surgical kernel, open joint. One horse died, shrapnel in chest, wing, T.A. B4, 150 Bde R.F.A. 30 Division.	
"	4/10/16		Evacuated 28 horses & 1 mule to collecting M.V.S. at MEAULTE.	
"	5/10/16		Evacuated 10 horses & 1 mule to collecting M.V.S. at MEAULTE.	
"			Destroyed 1 H.D. belonging to No. 4 Coy. A.S.C. shrapnel wound, fracture scapula at collecting M.V.S. at MEAULTE was horse. No. S.E. 8382 Pte C. BENSTEAD	
"	6/10/16		and No. S.E. 5045 Pte F. BARNES returned from the collecting M.V.S. at MEAULTE.	
"	7/10/16		Discharged one horse to 30 By. 39 Bde R.F.A. 1 Division, with slough joint.	

WAR DIARY or INTELLIGENCE SUMMARY

Army Form C. 2118.

Place	Date	Hour	Summary of Events and Information	Remarks and references to Appendices
MAMETZ	7/10/16	2pm 9/1st	Evacuated 37 horses to No.1 Vet. Hospital FORGES-LES-EAUX	
"	8/10/16		Destroyed one horse belonging to B.Bty. 9th Bde. R.F.A. 21st Division. Fractured Radius. Discharged one horse to H.Q.D.W. M.M.P. Came under N.H. cmdt.	
"	9/10/16		Evacuated 36 horses & mule to No.1 Vet. Hospital FORGES-LES-EAUX. Destroyed one horse belonging to D. Bty. 183 Bde R.F.A. Sprained wound. Fractured Pelvis.	
"	10/10/16		Evacuated 31 horses & mule to No.1 Vet. Hospital FORGES-LES-EAUX. Discharged one horse to C. Bty. 187 Bde R.F.A. Cured (Picked from.)	
"	12/10/16		Destroyed one mule belonging to 5 Bty. 2 Bde N.F.A. Sprained, Fractured Radius. Evacuated 50 & 6 horses (No.1 Vet. Hospital FORGES-LES-EAUX Sprained)	
"	13/10/16		Evacuated 48 horses to No.1 Vet. Hospital FORGES-LES-EAUX. Discharged one horse belonging to D.Bty. 93 Bde. 21st Division, Serum Sensit. 13 horses were sent to 14th NORTHUMBRIA M.V.S. for Evacuation.	
"	14/10/16		1 horse was sent new to H.Q. 15th M.V.S. 30th Division for Evacuation. 20 horses were sent new to 21st M.V.S. 9th Division for Evacuation. 20 horses were sent new to 23rd M.V.S. 12th Division for Evacuation. 20 horses were sent new to 27th M.V.S. 15th Division for Evacuation.	

WAR DIARY
or
INTELLIGENCE SUMMARY.
(Erase heading not required.)

Army Form C. 2118.

Place	Date	Hour	Summary of Events and Information	Remarks and references to Appendices
		3rd Fleet		
MAMETZ	15.10.16		One section left MAMETZ and marched to BUIRE-SUR-L'ANCRE and bivouacked for the night outside the village.	
BUIRE-SUR-L'ANCRE	16.10.16		The section left BUIRE-SUR-L'ANCRE marching under orders of the 12th Infantry Brigade and proceeded to ARGŒUVES and bivouacked for the night.	
ARGŒUVES	17/18.10.16		Discharged 6 stray horses & mules stray cable to 18th K.R. Rifles 1 2.0 H.y. Bde. The section left ARGŒUVES and marched to LONGPRE-LES-CORPS SAINTS and billetted in the town.	
LONGPRE	18.10.16		No. S.E. 8390 Pte. G. HAYNES returned to section from hospital	
	19.10.16		No. S.E. 12859 Cpl. L. M. MINTY was posted to No. 2 Vet. Hospital HAYDE for duty.	
	20.10.16		The section proceeded by rail from LONGPRE to CAESTRE entraining at 10.30 P.M.	
CAESTRE	21.10.16		Arrived CAESTRE station 10.30 A.M. and marched to FLÊTRE where men & horses were billetted for 2 nights.	

Army Form C. 2118.

WAR DIARY
or
INTELLIGENCE SUMMARY.
(Erase heading not required.)

Instructions regarding War Diaries and Intelligence Summaries are contained in F. S. Regs., Part II. and the Staff Manual respectively. Title pages will be prepared in manuscript.

Place	Date	Hour	Summary of Events and Information	Remarks and references to Appendices
FLÊTRE	23.10.16		4th Sect. 1st Lieut. on section marched to a M.V.S. camp near RENINGHERST, map reference G 32 D 8 1	
RENINGHELST	24.10.16	9 am	Got into the camp first 1st Australian M.V.S. including 120 horses and 12 mules	
"	25.10.16		Destroyed one horse belonging to 143rd B.G. 11"A.F.A. Bde 1st Australian Division not opened junt - off Antwerp	
	26.10.16	9.10 am	Iki H. was O/C lynn'd to No 13 Vet. hospital at NEUFCHATEL.	

C W B Wilkes
Capt. A.V.C.
O.C. 32nd Mobile Veterinary Section

Army Form C. 2118.

52nd Mobile Vety Section

Vol 6

WAR DIARY
or
INTELLIGENCE SUMMARY.
(Erase heading not required.)

Instructions regarding War Diaries and Intelligence Summaries are contained in F. S. Regs., Part II. and the Staff Manual respectively. Title pages will be prepared in manuscript.

Place	Date	Hour	Summary of Events and Information	Remarks and references to Appendices
REMINGHELST G.32.d.8.1	1.11.16		1st Sheet	
"	2.11.16		One horse of 37 Battery 10th A.FA Bde, 4 Australian Division was destroyed. Fractured Humerus. 4 horses and 3 mules were evacuated by road to No 23 Vety Hosp. at DMER. 5 horses and 6 mules were evacuated by rail from WIPPENHOEK siding to No 13 Vety. Hosp. NEUFCHATEL	
"	8.11.16		29 horses were evacuated by road to No 23 Vety Hosp. at SOMER	
"	9.11.16		Bull THEE B. S.E 5335 was admitted to 140th Field Ambulance and wounded the same day	
"	11.11.16		S.E 1514 Pvte 26 H.A.Y. was admitted to 140th Field Ambulance. 1 horse of Head Qrs 105 I.H.A. F.A Bde. 4 Australian Division was destroyed. Fractured Tibia.	
"	13.11.16		17 horses and 1 mule were evacuated by road from WIPPENHOEK Siding to No 13 Vety. Hosp. at NEUFCHATEL	
"	13.11.16		Duty for Major Knott A.D.V.S. of F.M. now 2.3.S- Remounts from the D.D.V.S. 2nd ARMY of HOPPOUTRE Siding. S.E 1514 Private HAY was discharged from duty from 140th Field Ambulance.	

Army Form C. 2118.

WAR DIARY
or
INTELLIGENCE SUMMARY.
(Erase heading not required.)

Instructions regarding War Diaries and Intelligence Summaries are contained in F.S. Regs., Part II. and the Staff Manual respectively. Title pages will be prepared in manuscript.

Place	Date	Hour	Summary of Events and Information	Remarks and references to Appendices
REMINGHELST G32 b81	17/11/16		2 Horses and 1 mule were evacuated by rail from WIPPENHOEK. Sick to No 13 Vet. Hosp. NEUFCHATEL.	
"	18/11/16		2 Mules of D Battery 187/Bde. R.F.A. 41st Division were destroyed for Debility. 1 Horse of C Battery 190 Bde R.F.A. 41st Division was destroyed for Debility	
"	19/11/16		10 Horses and 6 Mules were evacuated by rail from WIPPENHOEK sick to No 13 Vet. Hosp. NEUFCHATEL.	
"	"		1/8 G. Bty: ILLINGWORTH was granted 10 days leave.	
"	22/11/16		13 Horses and 4 Mules were evacuated by rail sick from WIPPENHOEK sick to No 13 Vet. Hosp. NEUFCHATEL, which of course is N.E.E. as a shooting colliery	
"	28/11/16		9 Horses and 1 Mule were evacuated by rail from WIPPENHOEK sick to No 13 Vet. Hosp. at ST OMER.	
"	29/11/16		No. S.E.9161 Private Wheatley A.V.C. joined the Section from No 12 Veterinary Hospital NEUFCHATEL.	
"	"		6 Horses by rail to No 33 Vet.y Hosp't at S.T OMER. Evacuated sick	
"	30/11/16		1/2 Corp. ILLINGWORTH returned from leave for duty	

J. Ross. Lieut
O.C. 52"/142 Vety Section
A.V.C.

T2134. Wt. W708—776. 500000. 4/15. Sir J. C. & 8.

WAR DIARY
or
INTELLIGENCE SUMMARY.
(Erase heading not required.)

Army Form C. 2118.

Place	Date	Hour	Summary of Events and Information	Remarks and references to Appendices
REMINGHELST	4.12.16		No. 772 Sgt. B. LONG granted 10 days leave	
GBNS.1	8.12.16		Evacuated 35 horses Emer's 2 mules to No. 23 Veterinary Hospital	
	9.12.16		Col: W. B. Siites A.V.C. granted 10 days leave	
			Lieut A.L.S. REYNOLDS A.V.C. took over command of the section	
			No. 5803 Pte. F. COVEY, 11 Queens R.W. Surry Rgt. attached as servant to Lt. REYNOLDS	
			No. SE. 8381 Pte. C. BENSTEAD returned from leave	
	11.12.16		No. SE. 8391 Pte. S.A. JEFFERIES granted 10 days leave	
	13.12.16		Evacuated 109 horses and 3 mules to No. 33 Veterinary Hospital	
	16.12.16		No. 772 Sgt. B. LONG returned from leave	
	18.12.16		No. SE. 5080 Cpl. E.R. SMITH granted 10 days leave	
	19.12.16		No. SE. 15143 Pte. S.E. HAY was admitted to Divisional Rest Station	
	20.12.16		Evacuated 50 horses to No. 33 Veterinary Hospital	
			Col. W.B. Suites returned from leave & assumed command of section	
			Lieut A.L.S. REYNOLDS A.V.C. returned to + 123 Brigade	
			No. 5803 Pte F. COVEY R.W. Surry Rgt. was sent back to Brigade	
			Destroyed one horse 1/B. Bat. 189 Bde. R.F.A suffering from Poll Evil	

WAR DIARY
or
INTELLIGENCE SUMMARY.

(Erase heading not required.)

Army Form C. 2118.

Place	Date	Hour	Summary of Events and Information	Remarks and references to Appendices
			2nd Sheet	
REMINGHE 25.12.16	22 & 23.12.16		Destroyed the horse of Hd O/the H.Q.d D.A.C. suffering from Pneumonia	
G.32.D.8			No S.E. 8391 Pte F.A. JEFFRIES returned from leave.	
	25.12.16		Destroyed no: mule 6113 Belgian Artillery with fractured ulna going to a severe & unredeemable damage done to the bicep. The Nr [?] of [?] [?] [?] of the stifle also conveyed roof of Man's [?]	
	27.12.16		Evacuated to No.23 Veterinary Hospital 39 mules cast I mule to No.23 Vet [?]	
			No.S.E.15142 Pte C.E. HAY discharged from 10 Can. Res. Veterinary Camp	
	28.12.16		No.S.E.3121 U/A L/Cpl W. OSBORN was granted 10 days leave	
			destroyed 1 horse of 1st Canadian Tunneling Co with Partial Paralysis	
	30.12.16		No.S.E. 3080 cpl E.P. SMITH returned from Leave.	

W.B. Okes
Capt. A.V.C.

WAR DIARY

INTELLIGENCE SUMMARY

52 Mot. Vly. Army Form C. 2118.

Vol 8

Army Form C. 2118.

Instructions regarding War Diaries and Intelligence Summaries are contained in F. S. Regs., Part II. and the Staff Manual respectively. Title pages will be prepared in manuscript.

Place	Date	Hour	Summary of Events and Information	Remarks and references to Appendices
REMING HEASTS JMY G32 D 8.1 Sheet 28		1 Sheet	Destroyed & buried one rmd H.B. Shrapnel argument (NH spring) belonging to 2nd Colonial Reserve Park	
			Two horses wounded in Tar Ambulance & 23rd Veterinary Hospital	
	3.1.17		No. S.E. 1383A Pte BISHOP A.V.C. got 10 days leave to ENGLAND	
	,, ,,		Evacuated 51 H. Cases and 5 mules by land to 23rd Veterinary Hospital	
	,, ,,		Evacuated 2 horses by land to 23rd Convalescent and 23rd Mobile Hospital	
	4.1.17		Destroyed & buried one Horse ? Pol. by A.S.C. 14 Division with (PARAPLEGIA)	
	,, ,,		Evacuation horses by land on ? to ? to 23rd Veterinary Hospital	
	7.1.17		Evacuated 2 horses by the Toc Convalescence to 23rd Veterinary Hospital	
	,, ,,		No. S.E.11171/80 Pte F.E. CHEALE A.V.C. attached from No. 4 Sec. L.A.H.S.A.C.	
	8.1.17		Evacuated ? camels to Tarc Ambulance & 23rd Vet. Mobile Hospital	
	9.1.17		Evacuated 5 horses by Tarc Ambulance to 23rd Veterinary Hospital	
	,, ,,		Destroyed & buried one mule? with ?? ? Rabbit the King by	
			2 Batty 13th BELGIAN Arty.	
			No. S.E. 6131 Pte OSBORN A.V.C. returned from leave	
	10.1.17		No. S.E. 5036 Pte BEATTIE A.V.C got 14. 16 days leave to ENGLAND	

Army Form C. 2118.

Instructions regarding War Diaries and Intelligence Summaries are contained in F. S. Regs., Part II. and the Staff Manual respectively. Title pages will be prepared in manuscript.

WAR DIARY
or ~~INTELLIGENCE SUMMARY.~~
(Erase heading not required.)

Place	Date	Hour	Summary of Events and Information	Remarks and references to Appendices
REMINGHELST HOSP. G.3. L.8.1. Sheet 28			19/11/17 2nd Lt. 5. L. Crisis R.A.M.C. returned to duty at 8.30 p.m. & was transferred to 23rd Field Ambulance	
			Belgian Military H.D. with Gastritis. In duty 9.30 p.m. attd. 13th Belgian Military Hospital	
	13/11/17		2nd Lt. W. E. Rowland RAMC admitted Head Injury (Neurosis) taken by ¼ Bearer Coy to 13th Belgian Military Hosp.	
			No. S.E. 11171 A/Cpl. F. E. Heale RAMC attd. to No. 4 Solar ¼ B.A.C.	
			No. S.E. 11876 Pte. Bishop AMC not fit for duty on leave	
	14/11/17		9/1 ..... 2nd Lt. S. Assam (Polish Legion) 23 days leave to England	
	14/11/17		No. S.E. 6045 Pte F. Barnes promoted Lance Corporal —	
	20/11/17		2/Lt. H. Sanders proceeded on leave to 15th Bt. R.G.A. X Corps	
			..... Cmdr. .... effect changes of 15th 19. B66 B.E.F.	
			capt. B. Jno. Miles (Colonel)	
			No. S.E. 5056 Pte L. Beattie AMC returned to duty	
	25/11/17		No. 34865 Pte B. Rhodes 13th Motts Regt. attached as Camp Warden	
			XHV Hd. Division held Quarters	

Army Form C. 2118.

WAR DIARY
or
INTELLIGENCE SUMMARY.
(Erase heading not required.)

Instructions regarding War Diaries and Intelligence Summaries are contained in F. S. Regs., Part II. and the Staff Manual respectively. Title pages will be prepared in manuscript.

Place	Date	Hour	Summary of Events and Information	Remarks and references to Appendices
RENINGHELST G.32.b.8.1	Jany 1917		3rd Report	
			No. S.E. 13817 S/Sjt Smith A.A. HARBOTTLE A.V.C. granted 10 days leave to ENGLAND	
	27/1/17		Evacuated 24 Canines by train to 23rd Veterinary Hospital	
	—		Evacuated 2 Horses by train ambulance to 23rd Veterinary Hospital	
	25.1.17		Evacuated 1 Horse + 1 Mule by train ambulance to 23rd Veterinary Hospital	
	28.1.17		Evacuated 2 mules by motor ambulance to 23rd Veterinary Hospital	
	29.1.17		No. S.E. 5377 Pte A.E. MORRIS admitted to 138 Field Ambulance	

C W B J W Rees
Capt. A.V.C.

WAR DIARY
or
INTELLIGENCE SUMMARY.

(Erase heading not required.)

Army Form C. 2118.

Place	Date	Hour	Summary of Events and Information	Remarks and references to Appendices
RENINGHELST	1/3/17		Discharged four horses cases to units	
G.32.b.81	2/3/17		Discharged one horse case to units	
"	3/3/17		No. S.E. 7636 Pte GRIFFIN A.V.C. granted 10 days leave to ENGLAND	
"	4/3/17		No. S.E. 1381/7 L/Cpl HARBOTTLE A.V.C. returned from leave	
"	"		Destroyed mule 1/15 R.W.KENT Regt, 123/28yr Bde, mule b.B.Bty	
"	8/3/17		Horse died of 5/2 Andrew's V/Infantry Section with R.Fusiliers 2 b.Bde 99 & Bde	
"	"		Grazed bole of 10 Middlesex Regt 123 army Bde	
"	"		Grazed bole of 10 Middlesex Regt 123 army Bde	
"	9/3/17		No. S.E. 8343 Pte BIBLEY A.V.C. granted 10 days leave to ENGLAND	
"	"		No. TS/10/70730 Pte Cpl GIBBS A.S.C. posted to No.1 Coy A.S.C. 41st Division	
"	"		No. T4/104014 Dvr BLYTHING A.S.C. attached to this unit from No.1 Coy A.S.C. 41st Division	
"	"		No. T5/SR/03773 Dvr WOOD A.S.C. returned to No.1 Coy A.S.C. 41st Division	
"	10/3/17		Destroyed mule Q/10 R.W.KENT Regt, 1/23 30y Bde, mule D.V.Bty	
"	"		Discharged one horse case to Major Carson D.A.C. 41st Division	
"	11/3/17		Bus. S.E R6. T4/210203040 Dvr to Maj Ramsdon, B.A.C. 41st Division	
"	14/3/17		187 Bde R.F.A. sent on duty to 3 Veterinary Hospital, one horse of B.B.Battery	
"	"		Evacuated 53 cases and to Mules to No.3 Veterinary Hospital of sick and injured equipment	

Army Form C. 2118.

WAR DIARY
or
INTELLIGENCE SUMMARY.
(Erase heading not required.)

Instructions regarding War Diaries and Intelligence Summaries are contained in F.S. Regs, Part II. and the Staff Manual respectively. Title pages will be prepared in manuscript.

Place	Date	Hour	Summary of Events and Information	Remarks and references to Appendices
RENINGHELST	15.2.17		2nd Lieut	
G32&21.	16.2.17		Discharged from Xmas a units for duty	
"	"		5 mules and 1 mule more sold for destruction (all B line)	
"	"		Evacuated 2 horses to No.23 Veterinary Hospital by Motor Ambulance	
"	17.2.17		No. S.E. 7632 Pte GRIFFIN, A.V.C. attached from line	
"	18.2.17		Evacuated 1 horse and 1 mule to No.23 Veterinary Hospital by Motor Ambulance	
"	19.2.17		Destroyed 1 horse of 10th B.W. KENT Reg.t/123 army Bde, both bowelly change	
"	"		2 horses sold for destruction, the B.inde, the Carries Arthritis	
"	20.2.17		2 Charge Stoppe re-transferred at RENINGHELST for treatment of	
"	"		Mange Mites, Scot: N.DIB A.V.C in Livery and 3 times fortnight	
"	"		Scottin. 21 to Aug is sent to with every sick horses from our unit.	
"	"		Capt. C.W.B. SILES A.V.C. admitted to 138 Field Ambulance	
"	21.3.17		No.S.E. 12824 Pte Bishop A.V.C. attached to 138 Field Ambulance (Servant)	
"	"		Evacuated 11 horses to No.23 Veterinary Hospital by road	
"	"		Evacuated 1 horse to No.35 Veterinary Hospital by Motor Ambulance	
"	22.3.17		Destroyed 1 horse J.C Battery 190 Bde R.F.A with ? acute Phlebitis	
"	23.2.17		Evacuated 2 horses to No.23 Veterinary Hospital by Motor Ambulance	

WAR DIARY
or
INTELLIGENCE SUMMARY

Army Form C. 2118.

(Erase heading not required.)

Place	Date	Hour	Summary of Events and Information	Remarks and references to Appendices
REMY GHURST G3.D8.1	3rd Oct		Battalion relieved by A. Bolt & 199 Bn. P.P.K. & unit. N.2.8346. P. Biddey A.V.C. returned from leave.	
			Arrived at & joined unit.	
			7.G.B.W.B. Stokes A.V.C. & C.S.M.S.M. from 132 Field Ambulance	
			No.S.E.1334 Pte B.S.Roback A.V.C. passes into a duty from 138 Fd Ambulance	
			and joined unit.	
			No.S.E. 3601 Pte Bartlett. A.V.C. granted 10 days Sick to England	
			granted 52 days on 3 Ambs at No.33 Stationary Hospital by Park	
			transferred in ambus to No.33 Stationary Hospital by Park Ambulance	

A.D.M.S. 1st Corps A.V.C.

WAR DIARY
or
INTELLIGENCE SUMMARY.
(Erase heading not required.)

Army Form C. 2118.

Instructions regarding War Diaries and Intelligence Summaries are contained in F. S. Regs., Part II. and the Staff Manual respectively. Title pages will be prepared in manuscript.

Place	Date	Hour	Summary of Events and Information	Remarks and references to Appendices
RENINGHELST $\frac{1281}{1381}$ G.32.b.81	1.3.17		Destroyed one horse of B. By 187 Bde R.F.A. with debility change	
			Destroyed one horse of A. By 190 Bde R.F.A. debility–Killed one allotted	
	3.3.17		Destroyed one horse 124 Bty R.G.A. acute arthritis (knee joint)	
	7.3.17		2 horses died at No 3 Vet Hos Kill– as sent to No 23 Veterinary Hospital	
	–		1 horse died at cavalry billet – A Army Reserve By R.F.A. reserve. Mo33 Veterinary Hospital	
			Evacuated 89 horses and 17 mules signed to Mo33 Vet– many empty ambulances by S. Vs Ambulance – to Mo33 Vet. 62 reported	
	8.3.17		3 horses died at No. 4 Dick Hall in sent to Mo33 Vet Hosp. inspected	
	–		4 ass died en route – at No. 4 Dick Hall and No33 Vet Hos. inspected	
	–		Evacuated by R.N. ambulance in buses sure – Mo33 Vetinary Hospital	
	13.3.17		No. 5:201 [?] T.W.BARTLETT returned from leave	
	–		Grazing 12 horses in area at 190 Bde – No33 Vetinary Hospital	
	13.3.17		Destroyed 1 horse of B. Bty 187 Bde. R.F.A. Bruised & displ.	
	–		Destroyed 1 horse D. Sec. H. M.D.A.C. Paralysed in Hind Q.	
	14.3.17		Destroyed 1 horse 233 Sec. R.E. debility $\frac{y}{3}$ Card	
	–		Destroyed 1 horse of 23 By R.G.A. Wasting illness and debility	

Army Form C. 2118.

WAR DIARY
or
INTELLIGENCE SUMMARY.
(*Erase heading not required.*)

Instructions regarding War Diaries and Intelligence Summaries are contained in F. S. Regs., Part II. and the Staff Manual respectively. Title pages will be prepared in manuscript.

Place	Date	Hour	Summary of Events and Information	Remarks and references to Appendices
REMINGHELST	14.3.17	3.19	2nd at rest	
Nr 28			Destroyed 1 horse of D.B+, 190 Bde R.F.A and 1 Sent sick & Evac. to Vet. Hosp.	
G 3.d.8.1			grouped in 30 2 mules of [?] sent to No. 3 Vet. my Hospital	
			grouped 2 horses [?] evacuated 2 mules by farrier amb & Evac. to No. 23 Vet. my Hosp.	
	16.3.17		Evacuated 3 mules by farrier amb & Evac. to No. 23 Vet. my Hosp.	
	20.3.17		3 Horses of D.B+, 190 Bde R.F.A &	
	21.3.17		grouped 1 Horse of [?] & 1 mule by farrier amb to No. 3 Vet. my Hospital	
			Destroyed 1 Horse of A.B+, 167 Bde R.F.A with Debility	
			Destroyed 1 Horse of D+, N.M. Police franskud Radeschungue	
			Destroyed 1 Horse of A.B+, 190 Bde R.F.A obtain [?] ev. To No. 23 Vet. ary hosp.	
			grouped 1 Horse of [?] 0 + 1 L.C.C.G. to No. 23 Vet. ary hosp.	
			2 Horses [?] use impaired 1 Sent with T.R.B	
	24.3.17		grouped 1 H [?] ams & 1 L.G. own Land of No. 23 Vet. my hosptl	
			Add 1 Horse of H.H. N.M.P. sent to No. 23 Vet. my hospital	
	25.3.17		Destroyed 1 Horse of 13 B+, 13 BELGIAN Artillery w/ moko, Debility & Pyrexia	
	27.3.17		Destroyed 1 horse of 11. R. Wheel Reg. Ll 123 days Bde. Extreme Debility	
			evac. 10 2 H'es by Farry Amb & evac. to No. 23 Vet. mary Hosp.	

WAR DIARY
or
INTELLIGENCE SUMMARY.

Army Form C. 2118.

Place	Date	Hour	Summary of Events and Information	Remarks and references to Appendices
REMINGHELST	27/3/17	3rd Sept		

WAR DIARY
or
INTELLIGENCE SUMMARY.
(Erase heading not required.)

Army Form C. 2118.

Mob. Vety Sec

Place	Date	Hour	Summary of Events and Information	Remarks and references to Appendices
REMINGHELST G.32.d.8.1.	3.4.14		No. SE/2913 Pte A. Guy, H. Hale A.V.C. evented to private for inefficiency evacuated 33 gassed and 3 mules by train to No 13 Veterinary Hospital	
	4.4.14		evacuated 15 horses by rail to No 23 Vety hospital	
			No SE/3439 Pte J.A. Stone A.V.C. absent at ...	
			... and found to ... in ... hospital	
			1 Pte J AVC ...	
	6.4.14		...	
	10.4.14		...	
			destroyed 1 horse extreme debility 1.189 Brigade AFA	
			... 1 ... ... ambulance ... 1.55 Brigade	
			Pte W. Austin R.F.A. admitted to 135 Field Ambulance	
			Pte T4/104014 Dr O. Blything A.S.C. returned to No 1 Sy Divisional Train	
			" T4/097168 " A. Parkes A.S.C. attached from No 1 Sy Divisional Train	
	21.4.14		destroying 1 horse ... debility 1190 Brig ode	

WAR DIARY
or
INTELLIGENCE SUMMARY.
(Erase heading not required.)

Army Form C. 2118.

Place	Date	Hour	Summary of Events and Information	Remarks and references to Appendices
REMINGHURST			2nd D. Vet.	
G.32.d.8.1	14.4.17	11 A.M	Destroyed 1 mule with wounds. Evacuated (unserviceable) 1 R.D.K.C.	
	16.4.17		No 6.7129 Gnr W. AUSTIN R.F.A. Galang Infirm 138 Field Amb Galang Gunshot wound Tulse J Mules by Motor Ambulance to No 23 Vet Hosp	
			Castings 3/34 12 Evac cases	meta
	17.4.17		Destroyed 1 horse Exten Debility of 189 Brigade HLY Brigade	
			Destroyed 1 horse Exten Debility & Horse Deb Ulcer Thin Contacts, SHR A.F.A. 189 Brigade A.F.A.	
	18.4.17		Evacuated 2 horses sent to Lamba Exp one & No 3 Vet. Infirmary & Extr	
			1 Horse Sick to Dis. Inf. & Decandioctioes Given BAIZEUX	
	19.4.17		Destroyed 1 Horse Debility of 189 Brigade A.F.A.	
	20.4.17		Graded 1 horse and 32 mules by Motor Ambulance to	
			No 3 Vet In or Hospital	
			Destroyed 1 H.B. Inter with Septic Pneumonia of 189 Brigade A.F.A.	
	21.4.17		No 56110941 Pte J.A. WALTERS A.V.C. Evacuated to 30th Mob. Vet. Infirmary by Sick Amb	
	22.4.17		Destroyed 3 Horses Extreme Debility of 189 Brigade A.F.A.	
	23.4.17		1 Corporal and 3 men A.V.C. attached 61 X Wy 66 Mob. Vet. Infirmary detached	

WAR DIARY
or
INTELLIGENCE SUMMARY.
(Erase heading not required.)

Army Form C. 2118.

Place	Date	Hour	Summary of Events and Information	Remarks and references to Appendices
RENINGHELST			3rd Lieut	
G33 d & I	25/4/19		Sustained 8 casualties extra & Relief of 189 Brigade A.F.A. by 149th R.F.A. who arrived from G.35.b. Excellent Arrangements. Knew also mainly who of 1/[?]1st N.L.I. (T.M.) Bty & put into A.H.D.H.Q. No 55336 R.A. CRAIGIE N.E.L. 16 Cyclist Fusiliers admitted	A.H.D.H.Q.
	26/4/19		Buried all Bay Ridge	
	28/4/19		Ground full of mines & Sent ambulance to No 53 Retrain on Arrived also 29 more cases	
	"		Destroyed 1 Pale Lights Phenomena of 2 Canadian Bombing Battalion	

W B Wells
Capt A.V.C.

WAR DIARY
or
INTELLIGENCE SUMMARY.
(Erase heading not required.)

Army Form C. 2118.

Mot Vet Sec
Vol 12

Place	Date	Hour	Summary of Events and Information	Remarks and references to Appendices
G.32.d.8.1 REMINGHELST	1.5.17 2.5.17		One horse cast for destruction & DESCHILDRE FRÈRES, BAILLEUL Evacuated 27 horses sick & lame by train to No.23 Veterinary Hospital	
	5.5.17		3 men of 2.D. DURHAM Light Infantry attached for fatigue work (T.U. men) 1 man 2/28 Royal Fusiliers returned to unit	
			No.S.E.5987 Pte. J. WETSON A.V.C. granted 10 days leave to ENGLAND	
	8.5.17		Evacuated 2 horses by train disk & lame to No.23 Veterinary Hospital	
	11.5.17		Evacuated 1 mule by horse ambulance to No.23 Veterinary Hospital	
	13.5.17		Evacuated 1 horse by horse ambulance to No.23 Veterinary Hospital	
	14.5.17		No.S.E.5080 P/A/Cpl: F.P. SMITH A.V.C. attgdfrom 2 P/A/Sgt. & proceed 9.4.17 to Thirty Kent on miss under No.1 type	
	15.5.17		2 Men A.V.C. attached from X Corps House Div	
	16.5.17		No.S.E.5987 Pte J. WETSON A.V.C. returned from leave	
			Evacuated 21 horses and 2 mules by train to No.23 Veterinary Hospital	
			Obtained 1 horse by train crocked once & No.23 Veterinary Hospital	
			2 horses sold for destruction & DESCHILDRE FRÈRES, BAILLEUL	

Army Form C. 2118.

WAR DIARY
or
INTELLIGENCE SUMMARY.
(Erase heading not required.)

Instructions regarding War Diaries and Intelligence Summaries are contained in F. S. Regs., Part II. and the Staff Manual respectively. Title pages will be prepared in manuscript.

Place	Date	Hour	Summary of Events and Information	Remarks and references to Appendices
G 33 d 8.1 REMINGHELST	18.5.17		1 Amb. cast? Ords. sole for destruction to DESCHILDRE FRERES, BAILLEUL	
			M.S.E. 8390 Pte G. HAYNES A.V.C. granted 10 days leave to ENGLAND	
	23.5.17		1 Pair of Durham cart wheels returned to unit	
			Evacuated 3 horses and 1 mule by road to No 23 Veterinary Hospital	
	24.5.17		No S.E. 8131 U/P/A/ Cpl. W. OSBORN A.V.C. posted to H.Q. unit	
			Veterinary detachment	
			No. S.E. 5080 P/A/ Sgt. E.P. SMITH A.V.C. transferred to	
			No. 9 Mob. Veterinary Section	
	28.5.17		Issued 4 stores for kit bags — 2 horses at REMINGHELST	
			2 horses sold for destruction to DESCHILDRE FRERES, BAILLEUL	
			1 Pair destroyed unfit for retention. War horse sold	
	29.5.17		No. S.E. 8/3014 P.R. IRVING A.V.C. granted 10 days leave to ENGLAND	
	30.5.17		1 Mule died from suffocation — severe wounds	
			39 mules transported by party to No. 3 Vet. Hospital	
	31.5.17		Evacuation by Entrain 100 mules to No.3 Vet. Hospital	
			POPERINGHE. Over 13 horses also sent	

O.C. 52 Mob. Vety Section

A.V.C. O'Lehy

Army Form C. 2118.

WAR DIARY
or
INTELLIGENCE SUMMARY.
(Erase heading not required.)

Instructions regarding War Diaries and Intelligence Summaries are contained in F. S. Regs., Part II. and the Staff Manual respectively. Title pages will be prepared in manuscript.

5 — [stamp] Sheet 1 Vol 13

Place	Date	Hour	Summary of Events and Information	Remarks and references to Appendices
RENINGHELST G.32.d.8.1.	1.5.17		Orderly & and 2 front A.V.C. posted from X Corps Veterinary Hospital. Spare Sick to No 10 Veterinary Hospital.	
	3.5.17		1 Artif. odd 3 front AVC received from X Corps Mobile Vety Section.	
			Wo. SE 8396 Pte G. HAYNES A.V.C. returned from leave.	
	4.5.17		1 N.C.O. and 1 Rank sent for Instruction to 5 DESCHINDRE, FRÈRE, BAILLEUL.	
	5.5.17		Destroyed 1 horse & 10 Pt. W. Seymour Rgt. 13th Army Bde. Wounds Suspired. Destroyed 1 horse of 116 B.H. 26 A.F.A. Bde. Company & and Debility. No. T.4/094188 D3/SS WATKINS A.S.C. granted 10 days leave to ENGLAND. Evacuated 14 horses & 1 mule injured to 33 Veterinary Hospital. Evacuated 5 horses by trail. 1 Ex mules Mobile Vet Section. Evacuated 30 horses & 10 mules injured & 1X mules Mobile Vety Section.	
	6.5.17			
	8.5.17			
	9.6.17			
			No. S.E. 1501 Pte R. IRVING A.V.C. returned from leave.	
	11.5.17		2 horses sent for destruction to DESCHINDRE, FRÈRE, BAILLEUL. 1 horse destroyed 2 19 L/s Middlesex Regt. 1st Army Bde Fracturing Radius. 1 Arrif. & 3 front A.V.C. returned to X Corps Mobile Vety Section.	

WAR DIARY or INTELLIGENCE SUMMARY

Army Form C. 2118.

Place	Date	Hour	Summary of Events and Information	Remarks and references to Appendices
REMINGHELST G.33.d.2.1.	10.5.17	—	Evacuated 33 sisters to X roads M.D.S. Vet. Detachment. N.S.E. 1487 Pte R.H. REES A.V.C. granted 10 days leave to ENGLAND.	
	12.5.17		N.S.E. 7664 Pte S. PRIOR A.V.C. admitted to duty from No 8 Vet. Army Hospital.	
	13.5.17		Evacuated 8 horses & 1 mule to X roads Mobile Vet. Section detached.	
	14.5.17		Vet. Section Lieut. REMINGHELST transferred to LA CLYTTE	
LA CLYTTE			Vet. Section opened at LA CLYTTE & took over horses of N.Y.a.8.5.	
	16.5.17		No.T+109488 Dr S.J. WATKINS A.S.C. returned from leave & evacuated S.N. horses & mules to No.14 Mobile Vet. Detachment	
	17.5.17		N.S.E. 5131 Pte M.W. OSBORN A.V.C. absorbed P/A Corp: with effect from 25.3.17 (circular orders No 153. 2.15-6.1.17)	
	18.5.17		N.S.E. 178 P/A Sgt. O. FILLINGWORTH A.V.C. absorbed P/A Corp: with effect from 25.3.17 (circular orders No 53. 2.15-2.1.17)	
	—		Pte H. HALE A.Y.C. granted 10 days leave to ENGLAND	
	19.5.17		N.S.E. 4915 Pte H. HAZE A.Y.C. granted 10 days leave to ENGLAND	
	20.5.17		Bty 4466 I Driver G.III H.B.R.G.A. noted ailing & reported sick. Evacuated by Light Ambulance to No 3 Vet. Hospt.	
	21.5.17		No. T. T. 0324 S P/A Nos. A. WILLCOCK A.K.C. /and Section from No.10 Vet. Hospital	

WAR DIARY
or
INTELLIGENCE SUMMARY.
(Erase heading not required.)

Army Form C. 2118.

Place	Date	Hour	Summary of Events and Information	Remarks and references to Appendices
LA CLYTTE	21.6.17		9 Evacuated 69 horses & mules by road to No 23 Vety. Hospital. Evacuated 1 horse & mule by Motor Ambulance to No 23 Vety. Hospital.	
	23.6.17		178 P/A/S. Sergt. I. KILLINGWORTH A.V.C. D.M.V. section to join Mobile Vety. Hospital. Destroyed 1 horse & 1 mule. 23 H. Battery R.G.H. with fractious arm.	
	24.6.17		Evacuated 11 horses & 5 mules to a M.V.S. 5th Army at WIPPENHOEK. 1 horse destroyed. A. Battery 277 A.F.A. (Open Sit of Ord.)	
	25.6.17		Evacuated 5 horses to a M.V.S. 3rd Army WIPPENHOEK. SE 54 59 P/A Coy? STONE & H.A.V.C. granted 10 days leave to ENGLAND.	
	26.6.17		Destroyed 1 horse of 181 Brigade R.F.A. Open gunshot fract.	
	27.8.17		Evacuated 11 horses to 9th Corps Veterinary Detachment HILLE.	
	28.6.17		1 horse died of C. 3.2 A.F.A. Ingrum Stomach.	
	29.6.17		Evacuated 34 horses & 7 mules to 9th Corps Mobile Veterinary Detachment HILLE. Evacuated 2 horses by Motor Ambulance to No 23 Veterinary Hospital. Also 2 mules.	

(J.B. Stokes Capt. A.V.C.

War Diary
for July 1917
O.C. 52nd Mobile Veterinary Section

WAR DIARY
or
INTELLIGENCE SUMMARY

Army Form C. 2118.

Place	Date	Hour	Summary of Events and Information	Remarks and references to Appendices
LA CLYTTE N7a85.	1/4/17		The Section left LA CLYTTE and proceeded to BERTHEN and took over Camp R.21.b.1.3 from 33rd Mobile Veterinary Section and took over 10 Horses and 1 Mule issued to 1/2 LONDON M.G. Batty. Sector S.E. 4913 Pt. HALE returning from say from 19. Middlesex Pioneers. 2 Horses and 1 Mule issued to 19. Middlesex Pioneers.	
BERTHEN R21.b.13	2/7/17		2 Mules issued to 4/1 Dvr. Cycl. Bry. 1 Mule issued to 19. Middlesex Pioneers.	
	4/7/17		Took over 11 Horses from 33rd Mobile Veterinary Section. Evacuated 13 Horses by road to No.23 Veterinary Hospital. Pte RENTON granted 10 days leave to ENGLAND. 5208 Pte BENSTEAD admitted to 139 Field Ambulance 8382. 1 Mule and 2 Horses sent for duty to No 6 Sick Horse Half, STAPLE.	
	8/7/17		54.5.9 P/A/ W. G. H. STONE returned from leave fm. ENGLAND. 2.lin 3/20 DURHAM night staff. Veterinary is /unit.	
	11/7/17		No. SE. 105142 Pte HAY granted 10 days leave to ENGLAND. No. SE. 8382 Pte BENSTEAD discharge from 139 Field Ambulance to No. 23 Veterinary Hospital.	
	12/7/17		Evacuated 18 Horses & Mules by hand to No. 23 Veterinary Hospital.	
	13/7/17		No. 146 Staff/Sgt. ILLINGWORTH.O. A.V.C. moved to sector from No. 24 Veterinary Hospital.	

WAR DIARY or INTELLIGENCE SUMMARY

Army Form C. 2118.

Place	Date	Hour	Summary of Events and Information	Remarks and references to Appendices
BERTHEN R.21.b.1.3	17.7.17		2nd Lieut —	
	19.7.17		No S.E. 5368 Pte. RENTON returned from leave from ENGLAND	
	20.7.17		T/2/9418 Dr. T. DUNN A.S.C granted 10 days leave to ENGLAND S.E. 8643 Pte. G.H. RIDLEY and S/E 8390 Pte. G. HAYNES admitted to 138 Field Ambulance	
	22.7.17		1 looked ½ & 1 new A.V.C. returned to section from No.8 Sick Hall STAPLES.	
	23.7.17		Lt. BERTHEM # proceeded day to La CLYTTE. Return. N° a 85 & took over from no ½ LONDON Mobile Vety Section. Grounded horses & mules to 33rd Mobile Vety Section. Not yet in Sector. 1 new A.R.S.W. out & 1 new from 1/2 LONDON Mob. Vety Sector Occupied 2 stalls of Field Ambulance & 23rd Vety Section Hospital.	
			S.E. 15:142 Pte HAY.C. returned from 10 days leave	
	24.7.17		1 New N. 26 R. Fusiliers attached just in insist	
	25.7.17		1 New S.E. 238 2nd army attached for fortnight	

WAR DIARY
or
INTELLIGENCE SUMMARY.

(Erase heading not required.)

Army Form C. 2118.

Place	Date	Hour	Summary of Events and Information	Remarks and references to Appendices
LA CLYTTE N.7.a.8.6	24.7.17		3.00 p.m. Q. Lt. W.B. Sykes A.V.C. given the Middle Sector to Capt. J.F. MacDonald. A.V.C. No. 12 & 14 Pk Pujab & 13 E. Surrey Regt attached as Grooms to O.C.	
	25.7.17		Capt. J.F. MacDonald A.V.C. granted 10 days leave to ENGLAND.	
	26.7.17		Evacuated 24 horses by train to 23 Veterinary Hospital	
	27.7.17		Evacuated 11 horses to D.D.R. Service Army S.E. 86 43 Pte RIDLEY G.H. joins 136 Field Ambulance	
	28.7.17		Evacuated 16 horses & 6 mules to 3rd Army M.V.S. Very Destructive – WIPPENHOEK. destroyed – of No. 1 Cny H.T.D.S.S. still reports to Horse SE 8390. Pte HAYNES G.H.T.C evacuated to N.4 CCS – Jaundice	

Army Form C. 2118.

WAR DIARY
or
INTELLIGENCE SUMMARY.

(Erase heading not required.)

Instructions regarding War Diaries and Intelligence Summaries are contained in F. S. Regs., Part II. and the Staff Manual respectively. Title pages will be prepared in manuscript.

Place	Date	Hour	Summary of Events and Information	Remarks and references to Appendices
Lt. CLYTTE N⁰ 4 E 6 29.7.17		4 R	1 horse destroyed by shrapnel wound of 11th Batt'y Austrlian F.A. Bde. Three sick horses for destruction to DESCHILDRE FRERES, BAILLEUL	
	30.7.17		1 horse sick for destruction at BAILLEUL	
	31.7.17		1 horse sick for destruction at BAILLEUL	
			To 19+18 B'd DUNN T. A.S.C. returned from 10 days leave.	N.J.B. Lt. i/c A.D.V.S.

WAR DIARY or INTELLIGENCE SUMMARY

Army Form C. 2118.

Vol 15

Place	Date	Hour	Summary of Events and Information	Remarks and references to Appendices
LA CLYTTE N16 85	2.8.17		2X recruits 23.8.L pass thro Amb. by road to No 38 Casualty Clearing Hospital. 2 mses destroyed of 38 Bn. 10 Brs Subway FA Fuschias and Dog advanced and back way established at H30 d 18. 1 mse C.P. for destructn to BESCHILDRE FRERE	
	3.8.17		1 mse C.P. to BAILLEUL between YPRES & DICKEBUSCH. An Ambulance killed. Gave it Dr Dine. Obliged to leave it at Dine.	
	4.8.17		11 mses T10 Rues evacuated to 3 Dups. Months Details enemy WIPPENHOEK, A.F.A. Bgd 1. A hostile air raid destroyed 8/13 By had. 1 mse orcuseen of 139 (F.1) A. hostile aeroplane dropped small fire bomb for destrectn at BAILLEUL 1 mse J.F. MACDONALD returned from sick leave. Cpl. ... 8395 Pte BROWN. M.S. returned from 10 days leave	

Army Form C. 2118.

WAR DIARY
or
INTELLIGENCE SUMMARY.
(Erase heading not required.)

J.... Sheet:

Instructions regarding War Diaries and Intelligence
Summaries are contained in F. S. Regs., Part II.
and the Staff Manual respectively. Title pages
will be prepared in manuscript.

Place	Date	Hour	Summary of Events and Information	Remarks and references to Appendices
La Clytte: M.17.a.8.5.	7.8.17.		1 horse destroyed of A Dye Cy: Royal Monmouth Engineers: fractured Radius.	
			5 men from X" Corps M.V.D. attached for duty.	
	8.8.17.		The advanced dressing tent moved to H.30.C.3.8. owing to hostile artillery fire.	
	9.8.17.		20 horses & 6 mules evacuated by road to 23 VETERINARY HOSPITAL. ST. OMER.	
	10.8.17.		1 horse destroyed of 233 Coy. R.E.: Shell wounds N.F. & head.	
	13.8.17.		1 horse destroyed of 28" A.F.A. Open joint N.H.	
			1 horse destroyed of D/47 R.F.A.: 4" Div: Laminitis & old age.	
			1 horse died of 47" D.A.C. No. 2. Sectn: Shell wounds Shoulder.	
	14.8.17.		1 horse destroyed of 17" Heavy Batt: R.G.A. Shell wound off shoulder.	
			3 men from 238 Employment Coy. returned to unit	
			4 men from X" Corps M.V.D. left with 50" M.V.S.	
			S.E. 3201. Pte. T.W. BARTLETT returned to X" Corps, M.V.D.	
			24 horses & 11 mules & 8 hides evacuated to 50" M.V.S.	
			The section left LA CLYTTE, & proceeded to BERTHEN, & took over camp R.21.6.13. from 50" M.V.S.	
			Men of the section billeted in barn.	
BERTHEN: R.21.6.13.	16.8.17.		Evacuated 20 horses & 1 mule by road to 23" VETERINARY HOSPITAL. ST. OMER.	

WAR DIARY or INTELLIGENCE SUMMARY

Army Form C. 2118.

Place	Date	Hour	Summary of Events and Information	Remarks and references to Appendices
BERTHEN	19.8.17		Evacuated 3 horses & 2 mules to X Corps M.V.D.	
	20.8.17		Evacuated 1 horse to X Corps. M.V.D. The section left BERTHEN & proceeded to P.O.W. camp near HONDEGHEM.	
	21.8.17		March continued to WIZERNES.	
WIZERNES	27.8.17		Evacuated 10 horses by road to No. 23 Veterinary Hospital.	
	29.8.17		All mares inspected by Major Herbert. X Corps. One mare selected for breeding purposes & branded.	

J.T. Macdonald. Capt: A.V.C.
O.C. 52nd M.V.S.

Army Form C. 2118.

WAR DIARY
or
INTELLIGENCE SUMMARY.
(Erase heading not required.)

Instructions regarding War Diaries and Intelligence Summaries are contained in F.S. Regs., Part II. and the Staff Manual respectively. Title pages will be prepared in manuscript.

Vol 16

Place	Date	Hour	Summary of Events and Information	Remarks and references to Appendices
MIZERNES	1.9.17.		Evacuated 14 horses & 2 mules to No. 23. Veterinary Hospital by road.	
	2.9.17.		S.S. 9441 Pte. MACKENZIE. A. joined section from No. 14 Veterinary Hospital.	
	8.9.17.		Evacuated 10 horse to No. 23 Veterinary Hospital by road.	
	11.9.17.		Evacuated 3 horses to No. 23 do do do	
	12.9.17.		Evacuated 8 horses do do by float.	
	13.9.17.		No. 178 Staff Sergeant ILLINGWORTH. O. proceeded on 28 days leave to England.	
	14.9.17.		Section marched to Sheet. 21. O. 34. 6.4.7.	
BERTHEN	15.9.17.		Section marched to BERTHEN. R. 21. 6.13. Sheet. 27.	
			One horse evacuated to No. 8 Sick Horse Halt.	
LA CLYTTE	16.9.17.		Section marched to LA CLYTTE. & encamped at N.Y.A.4.1. Sheet. 28.	
			T4/044188 Driver WATKINS S.J. A.S.C. admitted to 56th D.R.S.	
	17.9.17.		No horse on Infantry Brig. H.Q. destroyed. Fractured pelvic bone.	

Army Form C. 2118.

WAR DIARY
or
INTELLIGENCE SUMMARY.

(Erase heading not required.)

Second

Instructions regarding War Diaries and Intelligence Summaries are contained in F. S. Regs., Part II. and the Staff Manual respectively. Title pages will be prepared in manuscript.

Place	Date	Hour	Summary of Events and Information	Remarks and references to Appendices
LA CLYTTE	22.9.17.		21 horses & 3 mules evacuated by road to No.23 Veterinary Hospital.	
	23.9.17.		Evacuated 2 horses by road & 1 horse by float to X Corps M.V.D.	
	24.9.17.		Evacuated 2 horses & 6 mules to 50th M.V.S.	
			The section marched to CAESTRE & took over camp from 33rd M.V.S. at Q.32.c.1.6. Sheet 27.	
			J.2. 50.b. Pte. Beattie J. & J.2.8391 Pte. Jeffries J.A. rejoined section from X Corps M.V.D.	
CAESTRE			1 horse taken over from 33rd M.V.S. came from Sick of flock.	
	25.9.17.		J.2.6121 Cpl. OSBORN. W.W. & J.2.5201 Pte. BARTLETT T.W. rejoined section from X Corps M.V.D.	
	26.9.17.		Section marched to I.6.d.0.5. Sheet 27.	
	27.9.17.		Section marched to FERME POUSELTE. C.29.a.2.9. Sheet 19.	
LEFFRINCKOUCKE			Camp taken over in a dirty condition.	

(A7092). Wt. W12859/M1293. 75,000. 1/17. D. D. & L., Ltd. Forms/C2118/14.

Army Form C. 2118.

WAR DIARY
or
INTELLIGENCE SUMMARY.

(Erase heading not required.)

Instructions regarding War Diaries and Intelligence Summaries are contained in F. S. Regs., Part II. and the Staff Manual respectively. Title pages will be prepared in manuscript.

Place	Date	Hour	Summary of Events and Information	Remarks and references to Appendices
LEFFRINKHOUCKE	29.9.17.		Section marched to W.26. central. Sheet 11.	

J.F. Macdonald
Capt. A.V.C.
O.C. 59th M.V.S.

WAR DIARY
or
INTELLIGENCE SUMMARY.

Army Form C. 2118.

Sheet I.

Place	Date	Hour	Summary of Events and Information	Remarks and references to Appendices
N.26 Central: Sheet 11.				
	1.10.17.		Advanced Dressing Station established at N.18.d.2.7. Sheet 11.	
	2.10.17.		74/094168 Pte: PARKES.A. A.S.C. & S.F 961 Pte. WHEATLEY.R. granted 10 days leave to England. Evacuated 4 horses & 1 mule to No. 4. Vet: Hospital by rail.	
	3.10.17.		Corp: OSBORN & 3 men sent to XV Corps M.V.D. The section left N.26. Central, & marched to camp at LA PANNE.	
LA PANNE.				
	4.10.17.		2 horses & 1 mule sent to XV Corps M.V.D. for inspection by D.D.R. 4th Army.	
	6.10.17.		2 horses evacuated to XV Corps M.V.D. by order of D.D.R. 4th Army.	
	7.10.17.		Section marched from LA PANNE to camp at ST. IDESBALDE N.11.a.1.8. Sheet 11. & relieved 19th M.V.S.	

WAR DIARY
or
INTELLIGENCE SUMMARY.
(Erase heading not required.)

Army Form C. 2118.

Sheet 2.

Place	Date	Hour	Summary of Events and Information	Remarks and references to Appendices
ST: IDESBALDE.	8.10.17.		S.E.6395 Pte: Brown N.S. attached to 19th M.V.S. for duty. S.E.4787 Pte: Rees R.H. awarded 10 days F.P. No I.	
	9.10.17.		Evacuated 21 horses & 1 mule to No.4. Vet: Hospital by rail. 1 horse of 5th Batt: N.Z.F.A. destroyed (fractured tibia). 772 Sgt. B. LONG detached for duty at Divisional Clipping Centre.	
	13.10.17.		T4/094168 Dr. PARKES.A. A.S.C. returned from leave.	
	14.10.17.		S.E. 11664 Pte: JONES. J. granted 10 days leave to England. 178 S.S. ILLINGWORTH. A. returned from leave. S.E. 9161 Pte: WHEATLEY. V.A. returned from leave.	
	16.10.17.		24 horses & 2 mules evacuated by rail to No.4 Vet. Hospital.	

Army Form C. 2118.

WAR DIARY
or
INTELLIGENCE SUMMARY.
(Erase heading not required.)

Place	Date	Hour	Summary of Events and Information	Remarks and references to Appendices
H.T DESGALDE.			Sheet 3.	
	18.10.17		S.E. 4787 Pte. REES, R.H. returned to duty from F.P.	
	20.10.17		S.E. 9441 Pte. MACKENZIE. A. granted 10 days leave to England.	
	23.10.17		Evacuated 47 horses, 11 mules, & 12 hides to No. 4. Vet. Hospital by rail.	
	27.10.17		S.E. 7664 Pte. PRIOR. S. granted 10 th days leave to England.	
			S.E. 11664 Pte. JONES, G. returned from leave.	
	28.10.17		S.E. 5459 Corp. STONE. J. left section & proceeded to No. 2. Vet. Hospital to undergo training for promotion to sergeant.	
			S.E. 7664 Pte. PRIOR. S. recalled from leave by D.H.Q. wire.	
			S.E. 9441 Pte. MACKENZIE. A. do. do. do. do	

Army Form C. 2118.

WAR DIARY
or
INTELLIGENCE SUMMARY.
(Erase heading not required.)

Place	Date	Hour	Summary of Events and Information	Remarks and references to Appendices
St. IDESBALDE			Sheet A.	
	29.10.17		Evacuated 18 horses + 3 mules to 19th M.V.S.	
	30.10.17		Evacuated 9 horses to 21st M.V.S. S.E. 8395 Pte. BROWN. N.S. rejoined section from 19th M.V.S. Section left St. IDESBALDE, marched to LEFFRINKOUCK & took over camp at C.29.a.1.8. Sheet 19. from 21st M.V.S. Corpl. OSBORN & 9 men rejoined section from XV Corps M.V.D. S.E. 28932 Pte. DAVISON. H. joined section from base.	

J.F. Macdonald
Capt. A.V.C.

www.ingramcontent.com/pod-product-compliance
Lightning Source LLC
Chambersburg PA
CBHW081243170426
43191CB00034B/2029